Zaid Alyasseri

Introduction to Parallel Computing using Matlab

Zaid Alyasseri

Introduction to Parallel Computing using Matlab

LAP LAMBERT Academic Publishing

Impressum / Imprint
Bibliografische Information der Deutschen Nationalbibliothek: Die Deutsche Nationalbibliothek verzeichnet diese Publikation in der Deutschen Nationalbibliografie; detaillierte bibliografische Daten sind im Internet über http://dnb.d-nb.de abrufbar.
Alle in diesem Buch genannten Marken und Produktnamen unterliegen warenzeichen-, marken- oder patentrechtlichem Schutz bzw. sind Warenzeichen oder eingetragene Warenzeichen der jeweiligen Inhaber. Die Wiedergabe von Marken, Produktnamen, Gebrauchsnamen, Handelsnamen, Warenbezeichnungen u.s.w. in diesem Werk berechtigt auch ohne besondere Kennzeichnung nicht zu der Annahme, dass solche Namen im Sinne der Warenzeichen- und Markenschutzgesetzgebung als frei zu betrachten wären und daher von jedermann benutzt werden dürften.

Bibliographic information published by the Deutsche Nationalbibliothek: The Deutsche Nationalbibliothek lists this publication in the Deutsche Nationalbibliografie; detailed bibliographic data are available in the Internet at http://dnb.d-nb.de.
Any brand names and product names mentioned in this book are subject to trademark, brand or patent protection and are trademarks or registered trademarks of their respective holders. The use of brand names, product names, common names, trade names, product descriptions etc. even without a particular marking in this work is in no way to be construed to mean that such names may be regarded as unrestricted in respect of trademark and brand protection legislation and could thus be used by anyone.

Coverbild / Cover image: www.ingimage.com

Verlag / Publisher:
LAP LAMBERT Academic Publishing
ist ein Imprint der / is a trademark of
OmniScriptum GmbH & Co. KG
Heinrich-Böcking-Str. 6-8, 66121 Saarbrücken, Deutschland / Germany
Email: info@lap-publishing.com

Herstellung: siehe letzte Seite /
Printed at: see last page
ISBN: 978-3-659-69073-0

Introduction to Parallel Computing with Matlab

Table of contents

2

3

Preface

Matlab is one of the most widely used mathematical computing environments in technical computing. It has an interactive environment which provides high performance computing (HPC) procedures and easy to use. Parallel computing with Matlab has been an interested area for scientists of parallel computing researches for a number of years. Where there are many attempts to parallel Matlab. In this book, we will present most of the past, present attempts of parallel Matlab such as MatlabMPI, bcMPI, pMatlab, Star-P and PCT. Also, we will expect the future attempts. Finally, This book is for readers which have a basic knowledge in Matlab. I expect after reading this book you will able to solve any problem using Parallel Matlab.

Dedication

First and foremost, all praises to Allah the most merciful for the unlimited generosity and the guidance to complete this thesis. All praises to the prophet Mohammed (S.A.A.W) for whom his life and his track are the perfect guide for our life until the end of time.

Second, I would like to thank *University of Kufa in Iraq* for sponsoring my Postgraduate study. Furthermore, I would like to offer my deepest gratitude to *Prof. Rosni Abdullah, Dr. Mohd. Adib Hj. Omar* and all postgraduate students of Parallel Computing Architectures and Algorithms class from school of computer sciences at University Sains Malaysia for supporting this work.

Lastly, I am totally thankful for *my parents, my wife* and all members of my family and all my close friends in Iraq for their continued support. Although they are far from me, but they are always close to me by their love and passion.

1

Introduction to Parallel Computing

What is parallel computing?

Before defining parallel computing we have to know how the serial program running.The most of software has been written for serial computation. That means it is run on a single computer which having a single Central Processing Unit (CPU).Therefore, the problem will be divided into a number of series instructions. Where the execution of the instructions will be sequentially [1].

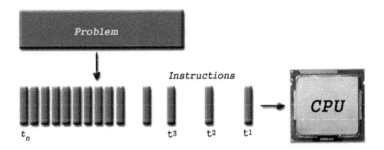

Parallel computing is one of the computing methods which execute many computation (processes) simultaneously. Where the principle of parallel computing is often can be divided the large problem intolittle pieces so that each piece can be executed at the same time (simultaneously) by using multiprocessors[2].

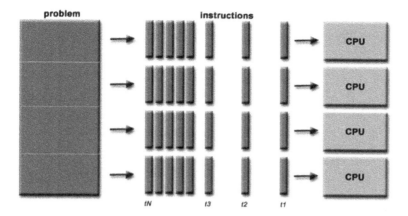

Figure 1 (a) and (b) shows how to divide the problem in sequential and parallel .

On the other words, parallel computing is the use of the multiple compute resources to solve a computational problem simultaneously . Which to be run on multiple CPUs.

In fact, the main advantages of parallel computing are :

1) Save time and/or money ;

2) Solve larger problems ;

3) Provide concurrency ;

4) Use of non-local resources; and

5) Limits to serial computing [1], [2], [3].

Computer Memory Architectures

In general, main memory in parallel computer hardware can be classified into three kinds: *shared memory , distributed memory and distributed shared memory.*

Shared memory is all processors interconnections with big logical memory (the memory is not physically distributed). Distributed memory refers to each processor has own local memory. Distributed shared memory combine the two previous approaches , where the processing element has its own local memory and access to the memory on non-local processors. Indeed, accesses to local memory are

7

typically faster than accesses to non-local memory [1],[2],[3]. Figure 2 illustrates architectural differences between distributed and shared memory

.

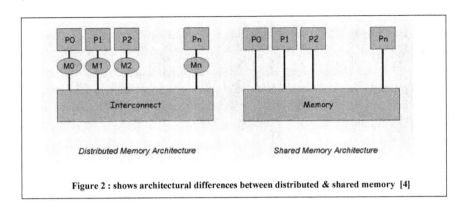

Figure 2 : shows architectural differences between distributed & shared memory [4]

Computer hardware architectures were developed rapidly for getting new benefits such as *power reducing, exploit all processors in modern computers* that contain more than one processor. On the other side, parallel computing software also evolved to achieve the advantages of parallel computing .One of the most important of these softwares is **Matlab** .Will address how Matlab language was developed to be compatible with parallel computing in the next section.

BACKGROUND ON MATLAB

Matlab is a numerical computing environment and fourth-generation programming language. Developed by **MathWorks** in 1984 and the newest version of Matlab is R2013a , Matlab allows matrix manipulations, plotting of functions and data, implementation of algorithms, creation of graphic user interfaces (GUI), and interfacing with programs written in other languages, including C, C++, Java, and Fortran[5],[6].

There are many advantages of programming with Matlab:**why Matlab?**

1) It's easy to learn and use where allowing non-experts to make changes and experiment;

2) It is fast and it has good supporting from (*http://www.mathworks.com/*) by tutorials and documents (*getting started*) and integrated help with built-in example code (help library);

3) It is interpretive and interactive and it has excellent debugging capabilities ; and

4) Matlab is widely used in academia, industry (almost one million users by some estimates)

But it is not free so you have to get licenses[7]. While Matlab is widely popular software used in many applications such as image and signal processing, control systems , statistical estimations, among machine learning community, financial modeling, and computational biology . Problems in these fields are computationally intensive requiring good processing power to solve the mathematical models within a reasonable period of time[8]. Where these applications need to be faster. Indeed, parallel programming using C/C++/FORTRAN and MPI is hard also creating parallel code in these languages takes a long time[9]. For these reasons, the scientists in MathWorks tried to apply the principle of parallel programming in MATLAB. In order to obtain benefits from the parallel computing to solve the big problems as fast and efficient. There are many attempts to develop parallel Matlab.

Where were developed a parallel Matlab

- **The MathWorks**

- **Massachusetts Institute of Technology (MIT)**

- **Ohio Supercomputer Center (OSC)**

- **Interactive Supercomputing Corporation (ISC)**

HISTORY OF PARALLEL COMPUTING WITH MATLAB HISTORICAL PERSPECTIVE (1995 TO 2011)

As previously mentioned, parallel Matlab has been an interested area for scientists of parallel computing researches for a number of years. There are many different approaches and attempts have been presented. Here will review the most important of these approaches.

The first attempt in this area for Cleve Moler, the original Matlab author and cofounder of The MathWorks, he has presented in 1995 "why there isn't a parallel in MATLAB" [7], where the author described three challenges in developing a parallel Matlab language: memory model, the granularity of computations, and business situation.

In that work, the author explained the most important attributes of a parallel computing like use shared or distributed memory. In this direction, Cleve Moler discussed the first attempt to make parallel Matlab in iPSC. It is one of the first commercially available parallel computers from Intel. The iPSC means "Intel Personal SuperComputer" 1985 , it consisted of 32 to 128 nodes arranged in an Ethernet-connected hypercube. Each node had a 80286 CPU with 80287 math coprocessor, 512K of RAM[7],[10]. Where each node could execute different program. One of the important points in Matlab which support memory model . There are no declarations or allocations because it is all handled automatically . The second challenge that was discussed in that work is granularity . The author presented an example of the Ardent Titan, where applied parallel Matlab on a *shared memory multiprocessor*. The third challenge is a business situation , where Cleve decided to make some changes in Matlab's architecture , at the same time, the author won't expect the appearance of distinct improvements in parallel programming in Matlab in the near future.

iPSC from intel in 1985

After *Cleve Moler* , there are many attempts to parallelize Matlab , but all of them faced   some problems. The most important problems that faced them are the parallel:

1) time in Matlab is not very attractive ;

2) there are a few resources in Matlab; and

3) the biggest problem is there were not enough Matlab users who wanted to use Matlab on parallel computers, but they wanted more focused on improving the uniprocessor Matlab [7]. However, The **MathWorks** and several Institutions did not stop at this point , but go on to develop parallel Matlab.

With the passage of time, several factors have made the parallel Matlab as one of the most important project inside the software development institutes because Matlab has become more widely used and it presented easy access to multiprocessor machines. Consequently, there are three approaches to develop parallel Matlab:

 1) translating Matlab into a lower-level language;

 2) using Matlab as a "browser" for parallel computations; and

3) extend Matlab through libraries or by modifying the language itself[6],[8].

The first approach is translated Matlab code into C / C++ or FORTRAN. Then will be parallelized the resulting code using one of parallel languages such as MPI or OpenMP, after that execute it on a HPC platform.

The second approach is to use Matlab as a "browser" for parallel computations on a parallel computer. While Matlab still does not run as a parallel ,in fact we cannot classify this method not more than a "web browser" to access to   parallel applications . This approach used from Intel Hypercube and Ardent Titan[6]. Now a commercial project called Star-P (*P).

Both of these approaches have significant limitations such as:

1) it's expensive ;

2) maybe it has an error-prone;

3) takes time ;and

4) it is very difficult where change Matlab code into C/C++ or FORTRAN it not easy and at the same time the modify it will be more difficult because single line Matlab correspond many lines in C language [6],[7],[8].

As a solution to these limitations , the third approach came , extend Matlab through libraries or by modifying the language itself. In this paper will be more focused on this approach.

Consequently, third approach there are two methods to develop parallel Matlab:

1) writing explicit code to perform inter-processor communication at the HPC platform such as MatlabMPI and bcMPI;

2) writing implicit code such as pMatlab, StarP and the Parallel or Distributed Computing Toolbox (PCT) or (DCT) [8]. We will describe all of them as following :

Parallel Matlab Programming Languages

MatlabMPI

It is a pure Matlab script implementation based on basic MPI functions[8]. It designed by *Dr.JeremyKepner* in the Lincoln Laboratory at Massachusetts Institute of Technology(**MIT**) [11]. Where the MIT Lincoln Labs are an implementation it based on six MPI standard functions [12] . The functions required for MatlabMPI as follows:

Function Name	Function Description
MPI_Init()	Initialize MPI
MPI_Comm_size()	Get the number of processors in a communication
MPI_Comm_rank()	Get the rank of current processor within a communicator
MPI_Send()	Sends a message to a processor
MPI_Recv()	Receives a message from a processor
MPI_Finalize()	Finalizes MPI

Table 1: Selected MPI functions provided by MatlabMPI[12].

This method has many advantages such as its use just the Matlab language for implementation. Consequently, it can be run anywhere Matlab available. The second advantage of MatlabMPI is that applies MPI communication of standard Matlab file I/O. Also this approach has a very small library (~300 lines) and is highly portable. The price for this portability is that the while MatlabMPI performance is comparable to C+MPI for large messages, its latency for small messages is much higher .

Finally, this approach has disadvantages, where requires a shared file system accessible by all processors. Where the system will face license problem for each node. So if its implements with shared memory machine only one Matlab license is required to run MatlabMPI. However, when MatlabMPI is run on a distributed system, such as a Linux cluster, a license for each multi CPU node is required[6]. *As a solution* for this limitation is to use intelligent compiler configuration tools for MatlabMPI that developed at Ohio Supercomputer Center (**OSC**) in 2006 [13]. Where these tools presented enhance to MatlabMPI by convert the MatlabMPI scripts which do not need Matlab licenses into alone executable then run them in parallel[13].

bcMPI

As we mentioned, there are several methods of parallel Matlab. The bcMPI is one of these methods. bcMPI is an open source software library, which is an alternative to MatlabMPI . bcMPI developed by the Blue Collar computing software   at Ohio Supercomputer Center(**OSC**) in 2006 to provide scalable communication mechanism and an efficient for development parallel Matlab also bcMPI is kept to compatible with MatlabMPI [9],[15]. According to,[8],[9],[15], there are several advantages in bcMPI such as :

 1) it has core library and separate MPI toolboxes for each of these interpreters Matlab (mexmpi) and GNU Octave (octmpi) ;

2) bcMPI has ability to work with large problem like Single Image Processing (SIP) problems;

3) it is compatible with MPI API ;

4) bcMPI has supports a collection of Matlab and Octave data types; and

5) bcMPI has been developed primarily on the Linux platform, but it has also been tested on the Mac OS-X, NetBSD and IA32 platforms.

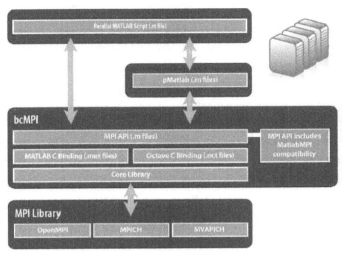

Figure 5 : shows bcMPI architecture [15]

Figure 5 illustrates the relationship between the various layers in the bcMPI architecture. Where the bcMPI has supported MPI functions and as summarize for MatlabMPI and bcMPI table1 shows the comparison between them.

Product name / function	bcMPI	MatlabMPI
tag values	integer values , but reusable	Random numbers or strings, must be unique
collective tags	optional, ignored	required
MPI_Bcast()	compatible with MatlabMPI	root does MPI_Send() to each process, receivers may call MPI_Bcast() or MPI_Recv()
MPI_Broadcast()	efficient use of underlying MPI_Bcast()	not implemented

Product name / function	bcMPI	MatlabMPI
asynchronous send	may block, unless user specifies sufficient memory size with MPI_Buffer_attach ()	never blocks, unlimited buffering using NFS files
MPI_Probe()	uses underlying MPI_Iprobe(), returns at most one pending message	returns all pending messages
MPI_Reduce()	supports any Matlab function with MPI_Op_create()	not implemented

pMatlab

pMatlab developed by Lincoln Labs at Massachusetts Institute of Technology (MIT) in 2004[8] . It is defined as a parallel programming toolbox which based on PGAS (partitioned global address space) approach [16],[17]. The pMatlab implemented an implicit programming approach   that gave several advantages such as: 1) It is supporting globalarrays for optimized performance by enable integrating between global arrays and direct message passing ; 2) It does not need any external libraries, where all implemented occurs inside Matlab; 3) that gave other good point is providing support for distributions and redistributions of up to four-dimensional arrays distributed with any combination of block-cyclic distributions; and 4) It is possible large data like SIP applications. Figure 6 shows the pMatlab layer architecture. pMatlabis used by default MatlabMPI communication library but for more efficient it can be used bcMPI[14].

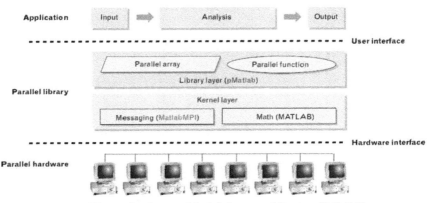

Figure 6 : shows pMatlab layer architecture[14],[17]

As we mentioned, one of the most important point in pMatlab is supporting global array. In fact pMatlab supports both pure and fragmented global array programming models. Where the pure global array programming model requires few changes in the code for providing the highest level of abstraction. In contrast, pMatlab in fragmented global array programming model provides guarantees on performance [14],[17].

Star-P

Another types of parallel Matlab is Star-P. Star-P Matlab developed at Interactive Supercomputing Corporation (ISC) in 2004 [8] . ISC launched in 2004 as part of MIT , in 2005 became an independent. Star-P Matlab is a set of extensions to Matlab. The main purpose of Star-P Matlab is to make the parallel of common computations are more simple. Where the Star-P categorize as client-server parallel computing platform in supercomputing , which has Matlab[18]. Figure 7 shows the architecture of Matlab Star-p where the Matlab will be as silent and the High Performance Computing platform as the server.

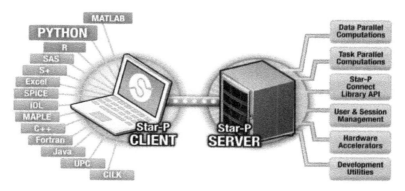

Figure 7 : shows the architecture of Star-p[18]

The approach of Star-P based on implicit programming where the kernel of star-P written using C++ language and MPI. The code of Star-P is like Matlab code just put *P for telling Matlab this code use Star-P for instance :

x=rand(2000*p,2000*p);

When Matlab gets *P, that means the next code uses Star-P type. The previous code will reserve x matrix 2-D (2000*2000) elements as random values to the parallel processor memory space[8].

MATLAB DCT and *MATLAB PCT*

Parallel Computing Toolbox (PCT) is the software introduced from the *Mathworks* in November 2004,(originally named Distributed Computing Toolbox™ and Matlab Distributed Computing Engine™, respectively but after that divided into Parallel Computing Toolbox and Distributed Computing Toolbox). Both Parallel and Distributed Computing Toolbox are based on the implicit programming approach[6],[8],[19] .

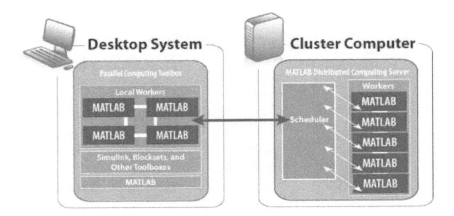

Figure 8 : illustrates the architcture of PCTand DCT [15]

Figure 8 shows the architecture of PCT and DCT, where the tools started allowing users to run up to 4 Matlab Labs or Workers on single machine[19]. In the version R2009a allows users to run up 8 Matlab Labs on single machine [18]. The version R2011b allows to use 12 users on single machine[19].

In 2008 MathWorks launched issuing Parallel Computing Toolbox as a separate product on Distributed Computing Toolbox[6],[19].

The advantages of PCT are supporting high level constructs for instance parallel for-loops and distributed arrays, it's has a lot of math functions, and it provides users utilize existing Matlab[6] .

Summary of history parallel Matlab

Finally, as summarized for these methods table 2 shows the analysis of these methods.

TABLE I. **ANALYSIS OF THE PREVIOUS ATTEMPTS IN MATALB PARALLEL**

Product name	Properties			
	Developed by	Year	Approach	Category
MatlabMPI	*MTI*	*2001*	*Explicit*	*Message passing*
pMatlab	*MIT*	*2004*	*Implicit*	*Partitioned global address space (PGAS)*
Star-P	*ISC*	*2004*	*Implicit*	*Client/server*
DCT	*Math Works*	*2004*	*Implicit*	*Message passing*
bcMPI	*OSC*	*2006*	*Explicit*	*Message passing,*
PCT	*Math Works*	*2008*	*Implicit*	*Message passing,*

CURRENT RESEARCH IN PARALLEL MATLAB

In this section will be focused on Parallel Computing Toolbox in R2014b especially Matlab PCT with GPU. At the end of this section there is discussion some of the benchmarks which solved using GPU and compare it with the CPU.

Graphics Processing Unit (GPU)

It were invented in 1999 by NVIDIA. A GPU is a highly parallel computing device. It's designed to accelerate the analysis of the large datasets such as image , video and voice processing or to increase the performance with graphics rendering , computer games[21]. In the last ten years, the GPU has a major development where it became used in many applications such as the iterative solution of PDEs, video processing, machine learning, and 3D medical imaging. The GPU has gained significant popularity as powerful tools for high performance computing (HPC) because of the low cost , flexible and accessible of the GPU[22]. Figure 10 illustrates architectural differences between GPUs and CPUs , the GPU has a number of threads where each thread can execution different program.

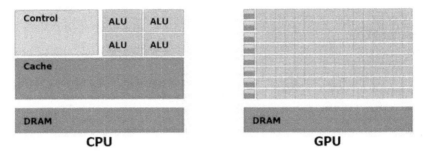

Figure : shows Architectural Differences between GPUs & CPUs [22]

Finally, the architecture of GPUs can be classified as Single Instruction Multiple Data (SIMD) .

Parallel Computing Toolbox (PCT) in R2012b

First of all, this version classified as the newest version of Matlab from Mathworks. It introduced in September 2012 . It has many new features such as : 1) supporting programming with CUDA NVIDIA for getting more advantages of GPUs; 2) supporting parallel for-loops (parfor) for running task-parallel algorithms on multiple processors ; 3) R2012b can be run 12 workers locally on a multicore desktop ; 4) for Matlab Distributed Computing Server (DCT) computer it supports cluster and grid; 5) interactive and batch execution of parallel applications ; and 6) distributed arrays and single program multiple data for large dataset handling and data-parallel algorithms[14]. Figure 10 shows how CPT R2012b run applications on a multicore desktop with 12 workers available in the toolbox, take advantage of GPUs, and scale up to a cluster with Matlab Distributed Computing Server [19],[23].

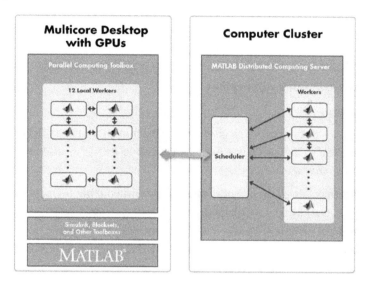

Figure : shows the architcutre of PCT and DCT in R2014b [19],[23]

2

Parallel Computing Approaches

Introduction

As we mentioned, in chapter one the main memory in parallel computer hardware can be classified into three types: *shared memory , distributed memory and distributed shared memory.*

Shared memory is all processors interconnections with big logical memory (the memory is not physically distributed). Distributed memory refers to each processor has own local memory. Distributed shared memory combine the two previous approaches , where the processing element has its own local memory and access to the memory on non-local processors. Indeed, accesses to local memory are typically faster than accesses to non-local memory.

This chapter content four sections. Section one we will describe the memory architectures, Parallel programming approaches will describe in section two, Flynn's Taxonomy will explain in section three, finally, some recommendation for designing parallel program will describe in section four.

Shared memory architecture:

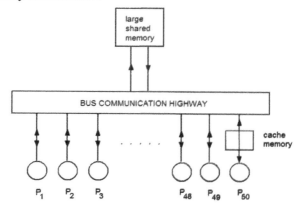

Figure1 : show the shared memory architecture

In this model the nodes share own local memory as one virtual global memory, that means, shared memory processors have a global address space which is accessible by all processors. A processor can communicate with another by writing into the global memory where the second processor can read it, for example, Processor one (P1) needs an information from Processor two (P2) so P1 will write into global memory and P2 will read the request from it. The communication process (read and write) is asynchronously. By the way the shared memory is controlled by access mechanisms such as lock/unlock. The main important point in shared memory model is the shared memory location must not be changed by one task while another concurrent task is accessing it. The advantages of shared memory architecture from the programmer's point of view is easy to program and faster than message passing architecture, but at the same time is difficult to understand and the scalability is limited by the number of access pathways to memory. Finally, example of shared memory is IBM ES-9000.

Message-Passing/Distributed-Memory architecture (MPI):

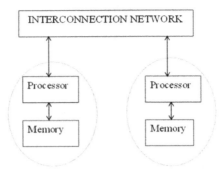

Figure 2 : show the message passing memory architecture

Distributed memory architecture of this model each processor has its own memory and processors are connected via interconnection network (figure 2). In Message passing , A processor can communicate with another by send and receive between them (we will describe Message passing communication types in chapter 3). There is a total of 125 functions in MPI, but one can write a fully functional MPI program using only 6 routines.

Need to know/understand the following:

- How to start and end the MPI library.
- Concept of communicators.
- How to get some information (size and rank of processes).
- Sending and receiving messages.

Figure 3   shows the communication process between two processors where P1 need some data which it in P2's memory, so P1 will request this data by using send commandSEND (x, P2) where x is the address of the datain P2 memory.

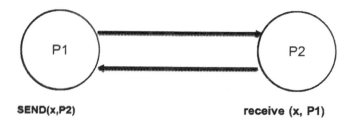

SEND(x,P2)   receive (x, P1)

Figure 3 : show the communication processin message passing memory
architecture

Table 1 : shows Basic MPI Functions:

Function Name	Function Description
MPI_Init()	Initialize MPI
MPI_Comm_size()	Get the number of processors in a communication
MPI_Comm_rank()	Get the rank of current processor within a communicator
MPI_Send()	Sends a message to a processor
MPI_Recv()	Receives a message from a processor
MPI_Finalize()	Finalizes MPI

Distributed Shared Memory (DSM)

The shared memory programming model is desirable but distributed
systems are scalable: A hybrid of both: DSM

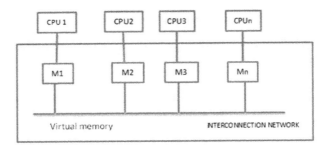

Figure 4 : show the Distributed Shared Memory architecture

DSM simulates a logical shared memory address space over a set of physically distributed local memory systems. An address-mapping scheme ensures that the entire distributed memory space can be uniquely represented as a single shared resource.

Some advantages of DSM:

- Hide data movement and provide a simpler abstraction for sharing data.
- Allows the passing of complex structures by reference.
- Cheaper to build than multiprocessors.
- Larger memory sizes are available to programs, by combining all physical memory of all nodes.
- Unlimited number of nodes can be used / scalable.
- Programs written for shared memory multiprocessors can be run on DSM systems.
- Ex: DREAM, Phosporus, TreadMarks.

Flynn's Taxonomy (1967)

A classification based on how the machine relates its instruction stream to the data stream

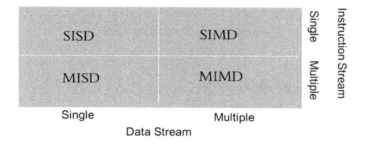

Single Instruction Single Data (SISD)

- A serial (non-parallel) computer
- Single instruction: only one instruction stream is being acted on by the CPU during any one clock cycle
- Single data: only one data stream is being used as input during any one clock cycle
- Examples: older generation mainframes, minicomputers and workstations; most modern day PCs. UNIVAC1, IBM360

Single Instruction Multiple Data(SIMD)

- A type of parallel computer
- Single instruction: All processing units execute the same instruction at any given clock cycle
- Multiple data: Each processing unit can operate on a different data element
- Best suited for specialized problems characterized by a high degree of regularity, such as graphics/image processing.
- Synchronous (lockstep) and deterministic execution
- Examples:

- Processor Arrays: Connection Machine CM-2, MasPar MP-1 & MP-2, ILLIAC IV
- Vector Pipelines: IBM 9000, Cray X-MP, Y-MP & C90, Fujitsu VP, NEC SX-2, Hitachi S820, ETA10

- Most modern computers, particularly those with graphics processor units (GPUs) employ SIMD instructions and execution units.

Multiple Instruction Single Data (MISD)

- A single data stream is fed into multiple processing units.
- Each processing unit operates on the data independently via independent instruction streams.
- Very rare class of parallel computer. One is the experimental Carnegie-Mellon C.mmp computer (1971).
- One potential use is multiple cryptography algorithms attempting to crack a single coded message.

Multiple Instruction Multiple Data(MIMD)

- The most common type of parallel computer.
- Multiple Instruction: every processor may be executing a different instruction stream
- Multiple Data: every processor may be working with a different data stream
- Execution can be synchronous or asynchronous, deterministic or non-deterministic
- Examples: most current supercomputers, networked parallel computer clusters and "grids", multi-processor SMP computers, multi-core PCs.
- Note: many MIMD architectures also include SIMD execution sub-components

Flynn-Johnson (1988) classification

MIMD computers can be divided into TWO broad categories:

1. Shared/Global memory.

2. Distributed Memory.

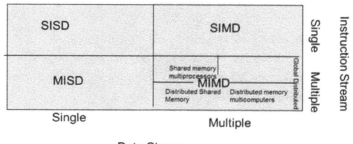

How to start designing a parallel program?

- You have to Understand the problemthat will be solved.

- Identify the parallelism in the problem. The most important question Is the problem parallelisable? If yes,so how can you parallelisable by data decomposition or functiondecomposition?

- Choose a programming model that allows you to express this parallelism- shared memory? Message-passing?

- Choose a language and hardware that together allow you to take advantage of the parallelism

- For each programming model that you select, reconsider design issues specific to the model.

3

Parallel Computing with Matlab

How to install Matlab on your computer

Before starting to install Matlab we should prepare some items with Matlab software such as File Installation Key and License File. We need these items to perform an off-network installation and activation.

Windows Systems — Get the name and password of the administrator account on your computer. The installer modifies the system registry during installation.

Select your new account type

Dell
Administrator
Password protected

You should
be as
Administrator

Step 1: Start the Installer

The method you use to start the installer depends on your platform.

Windows — Insert the DVD into the DVD drive connected to your system or double-click the installer file you downloaded from the MathWorks Web site. The installer should start automatically.

Step 2: Choose to Install Without Using the Internet

If you do not have an Internet connection, **select the Install without using the Internet** option and click **Next**.

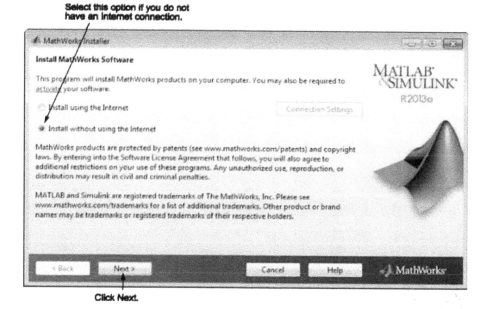

Select this option if you do not
have an Internet connection.

Click Next.

Step 3: Review the License Agreement

Review the software license agreement and, if you agree with the terms, select **Yes** and click **Next**.

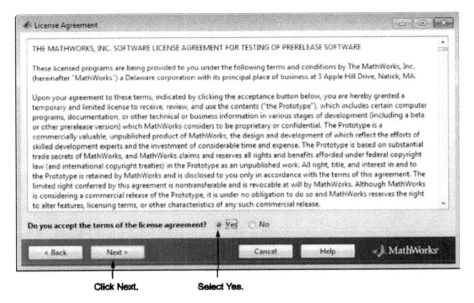

Click Next.   Select Yes.

Step 4: Specify the File Installation Key

If you do not have an Internet connection, and choose to install manually, the installer displays the File Installation Key dialog box. A File Installation Key identifies the products you can install.

If you have the key, select the **I have the File Installation Key for my license option**, enter the File Installation Key, and click **Next**.

The administrator contact on a license can retrieve the File Installation Key from the License Center at the MathWorks Web site.

If you do not have the key, select **the I do not have the File Installation Key option** and click **Next**. The installer will provide you with the information you need to get a key.

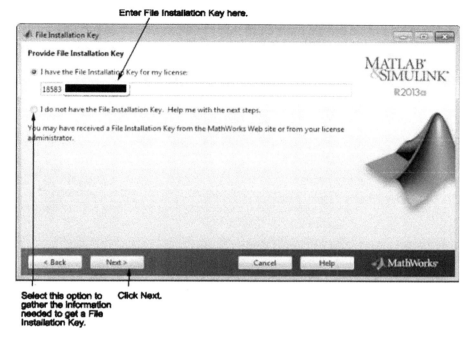

Enter File Installation Key here.

Select this option to   Click Next.
gather the information
needed to get a File
Installation Key.

Credit: http://www.mathworks.com/

If You Do Not Have the File Installation Key

The installation and Activation Next Steps dialog box contains the information you need to retrieve your File Installation Key from the License Center at the **MathWorks** Web site: http://www.mathworks.com/.

This information includes:

- Host ID
- Release number (for example, R2013a)
- Operating system user name (Note that user names are case-sensitive in activation.).

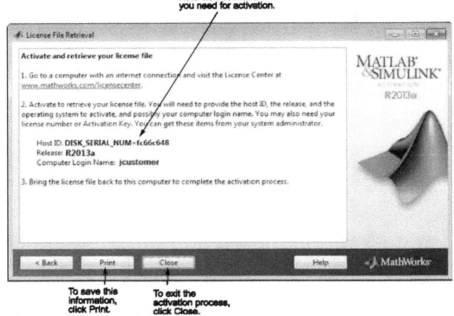

To get your File Installation Key:

1. Remember the information displayed in this dialog box and click **Finish** to exit the installer. On Windows and Linux systems, you can click **Print** to print out the information.

2. Go to a computer with an Internet connection and log in to your account at the MathWorks Web site.

3. Visit the License Center and enter the information from this dialog box. MathWorks uses this information to generate a File Installation Key and License File for your license.

4. Return to your computer and re-run the installer. With the File Installation Key and a License File, you can install and activate the software without an Internet connection.

Step 5: Choose the Installation Type

In the Installation Type dialog box, specify whether you want to perform a Typical or Custom installation and click Next.

Choose Typical if you have an Individual or Group license and do not need to specify which products you want to install and do not need to access any installation options.

Choose Custom if you need to specify which products to install, need access to installation options, or need to install the license manager (network license options only).

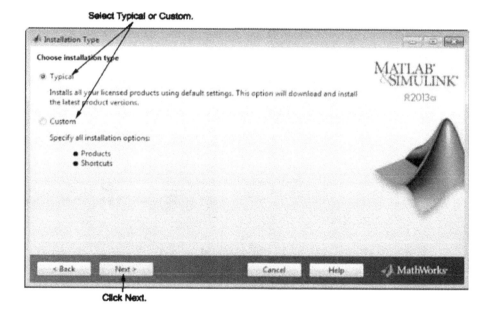

Step 6: Specify the Installation Folder

Specify the name of the folder where you want to install MathWorks products. Accept the default installation folder or click Browse to select a different one. If the folder doesn't exist, the installer creates it.

On Macintosh systems, the installer puts the MATLAB application package, *MATLAB_R2013a.app*, in the *Applications* folder, by default.

When specifying a folder name, you can use any alphanumeric character and some special characters, such as underscores. The installer tells you if the name you specified includes any characters that are not permitted in folder names. If you make a mistake while entering a folder name and want to start over, click Restore Default Folder. After making your selection, click Next.

Specify name of installation folder.

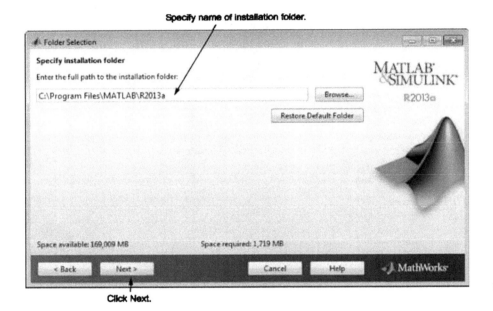

Click Next.

Step 7: Specify Products to Install (Custom Only)

If you are performing a custom installation, you can specify which products you want to install on the Product Selection dialog box. This dialog box lists all the products associated with the license you selected or with the Activation Key you specified. In the dialog box, all the products are preselected for installation. If you do not want to install a particular product, clear the check box next to its name.

After selecting the products you want to install, click Next to continue with the installation.

Click here to select or clear all product check boxes.

Select the products you want to install.

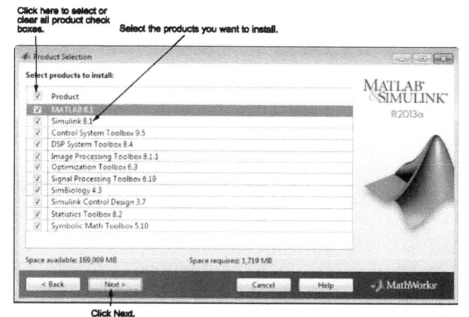

Click Next.

Step 8: Specify Installation Options (Custom Only)

For Custom installations, you can specify several installation options, depending on your platform.

Windows Systems

On Windows, the Installation Options dialog box lets you choose whether to put shortcuts for starting MATLAB software in the **Start** menu and on the desktop.

After selecting installation options, click **Next** to proceed with the installation.

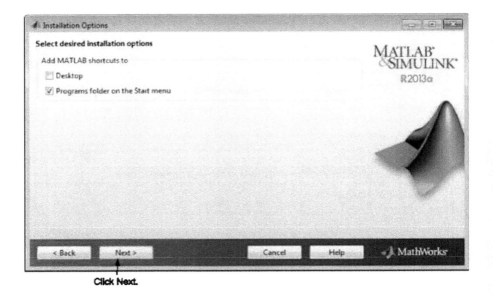

Click Next.

Step 9: Confirm Your Choices and Begin Copying Files

Before it begins copying files to your hard disk, the installer displays a summary of your installation choices. To change a setting, click **Back**. To proceed with the installation, click **Install**.

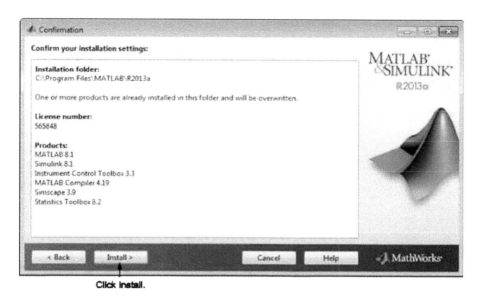

Click Install.

Step 10: Complete the Installation

When the installation successfully completes, the installer displays the Installation Complete dialog box. In this dialog box, you can choose to activate the software you just installed. You cannot use the software you installed until you activate it. **MathWorks** recommends activating immediately after installation. Click **Next** to proceed with activation.

If you choose to exit the installer without performing activation, clear the **Activate MATLAB** option and click **Finish** (the button label changes). You can activate later using the activation application.

To activate your software, leave this selected.

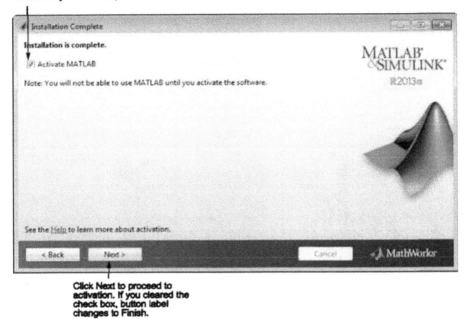

Click Next to proceed to
activation. If you cleared the
check box, button label
changes to Finish.

Step 11: Activate Your Installation

Because you were not logged in to your MathWorks Account during installation,
or you started the activation application independently, you must choose whether
to activate automatically or manually. Select the **Activate manually without the
Internet** option and click **Next**.

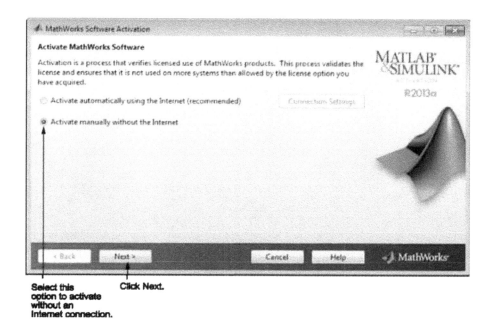

Select this option to activate without an Internet connection.

Click Next.

Step 12: Specify the Path to the License File

To activate without an Internet connection, you must have a License File. The License File identifies which products you can run. The administrator contact on the license can retrieve the License File from the License Center at the MathWorks Web site. Select the **Enter the path to the License File** option and enter the full path of your License File in the text box (or drag and drop the file) and click **Next**

If you do not have your License File, select the **I do not have a license file** option and click **Next** to get information about how to retrieve a **License File**.

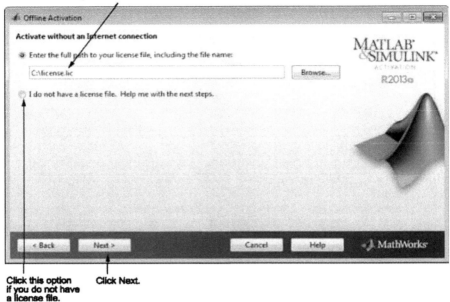

Specify the full path to
your license file here.

Click this option   Click Next.
if you do not have
a license file.

If You Do Not Have a License File

If you are activating manually and do not have your License File, the License File Retrieval dialog box explains how to get your License File and finish activation. The dialog box displays the information you will need to get your License File, including:

- Host ID
- Release number (for example, R2013a)
- Operating system user name (Note that user names are case-sensitive in activation.)

Save the information displayed in this dialog box. For example, you can print a copy by clicking **Print**. Take the information to a computer with an Internet connection and visit the License Center at the **MathWorks** Web site. MathWorks uses this information to generate a File Installation Key and a License File. You must have this information with you when you return to the computer on which you want to install and activate the software. To exit the activation application, click **Finish**.

Perform this procedure to complete activation.

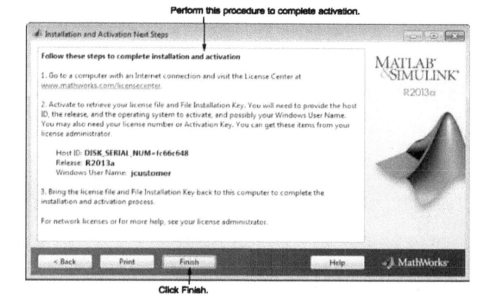

Click Finish.

Step 13: Complete the Activation

After activating your installation, click **Finish** to exit the activation process.

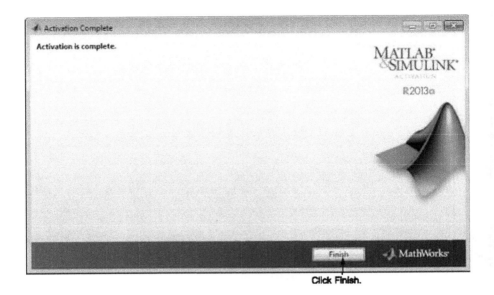

Click Finish.

How to start with Parallel computing using Matlab

Actually, Matlab's have five ways to parallelism:

1. Multiple Threads :The internal routines are written to explicitly support multiple threads and multiple cores.

2. Asynchronous Batch Mode : submit jobs to a worker pool

3. Single Instruction Multiple Data(SIMD): uses Matlab's **pmode** to perform the same instructions on multiple workers.

4. Distributed Matrices - built-in operations on matricesdistributed across multiple workers. This is actually MPI.

5. GPU - the most recent version of Matlab can use GPUs viaMEX les (C-code describing a GPU kernel).

We will describe all of them in basic Matlab example and try to parallelize it.

Example / How to find AB-BA (Matrix Algebra) using for-loops

That means we need to fine **A*B-B*A**

Sol/

```
C= zeros(N);

for i=1:N

    for j=1:N

        for k=1:N

        C(i,j) = C(i,j) + A(i,k)*B(k,j);

        end

        for k=1:N

        C(i,j) = C(i,j) - B(i,k)*A(k,j);

        end

    end

end
```

4

Parallel Computing Toolbox (PCT) in Matlab

Introduction

Parallel Computing Toolbox (PCT) is the software introduced from the Mathworks in November 2004,(originally named Distributed Computing Toolbox™ and Matlab Distributed Computing Engine™, respectively but after that divided into Parallel Computing Toolbox and Distributed Computing Toolbox). Both Parallel and Distributed Computing Toolbox are based on the implicit programming approach

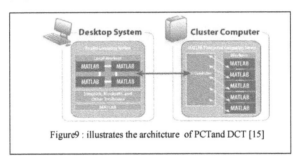

Figure9 : illustrates the architcture of PCTand DCT [15]

Figure 9 – shows the architecture of PCT and DCT, where the tools started allowing users to run up to 4 Matlab Labs or Workers on a single machine. In the version R2009a allows users to run up 8 Matlab Labs on a single machine. The version R2011b allows to use 12 users on a single machine.

In 2008 MathWorks launched issuing Parallel Computing Toolbox as a separate product on Distributed Computing Toolbox.

The advantages of the PCT are supporting high level constructs for instance parallel for-loops and distributed arrays, it's had a lot of math functions, and it provides users utilize existing Matlab .

Development of PCT

According to, MathWorks ,Table 1 shows stages of development in the Parallel Computing Toolbox (PCT) from 2006 until the first half of 2012 .

Matlab version	The new features of Parallel Computing Toolbox
R2006b	<ul><li>Support Windows 64 (*Win64*) for both Matlab client and worker machines.</li><li>*Distributed arrays are partitioned into segments*, that means will be more efficient use of memory and faster, where each segment will send to a different lab. Finally, each lab will be processed and store the own part.</li></ul>
R2007a	<ul><li>Allowing users to run up to 4 Matlab Labs on single machine.</li><li>New **pmode** interface and new default scheduler for pmode</li></ul>
R2007b	<ul><li>New Parallel for-Loops (*parfor-Loops*)</li><li>A new graphical user interface for creating and modifying user configurations.</li><li>Parallel Profiler.</li></ul>
R2008a	<ul><li>**Parallel Computing Toolbox support**</li><li>*parfor* Syntax has single usage</li></ul>
R2008b	<ul><li>**Matlab compiler product support for Parallel Computing Toolbox applications.**</li><li>Rerunning failed tasks.</li><li>Enhanced job control with generic scheduler interface</li><li>Composite objects provide direct access from the client (desktop) program to data that is stored on labs in the MATLAB pool.</li></ul>
R2009a	<ul><li>**A number of local workers increased to 8.**</li><li>Support Microsoft Windows HPC Server 2008 (CCS v2).</li></ul>

R2009b	• Support for Job Templates and Description Files with HPC Server 2008.
R2010a	• Enhanced Functions for Distributed Arrays • taskFinish File for Matlab Pool
R2010b	• **GPU Computing.** • Enhanced Functions for Distributed Arrays • Support for Microsoft Windows HPC Server 2008 R2.
R2011a	• **Enhanced GPU Support** • Distributed Array Support • Enhanced parfor Support. • support Microsoft Windows HPC Server on 32-bit Windows clients.
R2011b	• Number of Local Workers **Increased to 12.** • New Job Monitor • **Enhanced GPU Support where R2011b only support the latest NVIDIA CUDA device driver.**
R2012a	• **New Programming Interface** • Cluster Profiles • **Enhanced GPU Support**

Parallel Computing Toolbox in R2012b

First of all, this version classified as the newest version of Matlab from **Mathworks**. It introduced in September 2012 . It has many new features such as :

1) Supporting programming with **CUDA NVIDIA** for getting more advantages of GPUs; 2) Supporting parallel for-loops *(parfor)* for running task-parallel algorithms on multiple processors ;

3) R2012b can be run 12 workers locally on a multicore desktop ; 4) For Matlab Distributed Computing Server (DCT) computer it supports cluster and grid; 5) interactive and batch execution of parallel applications ; and 6) distributed arrays and single program multiple data for large dataset handling and data-parallel algorithms. The next figure shows how CPT R2012b run applications on a

multicore desktop with 12 workers available in the toolbox, take advantage of GPUs, and scale up to a cluster with Matlab Distributed Computing Server.

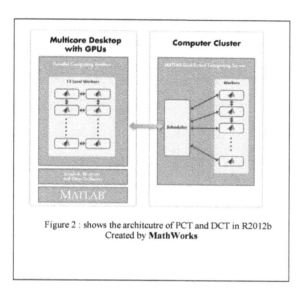

Figure 2 : shows the architcutre of PCT and DCT in R2012b
Created by **MathWorks**

Determining Product Installation and Versions To determine if the Parallel Computing Toolbox software has been is installed on your computer, please write " **ver**" this command at the MATLAB prompt: After that, MATLAB will display information about the version of MATLAB you are running, including a list of all toolboxes installed on your system and their version numbers. Figures 3 and 4 show a MATLAB version of your computer. Note that the toolbox and server software must be the same version.

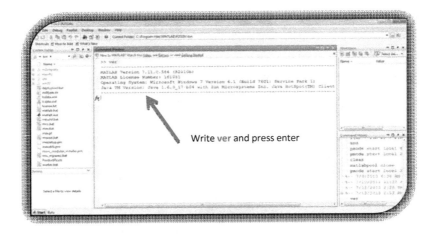

Write **ver** and press enter

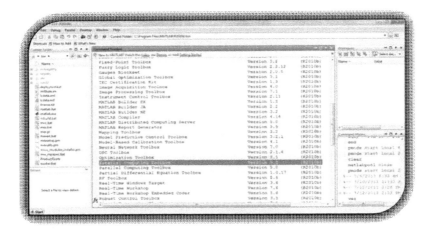

pmode

Interactive Parallel Command Wind

pmode start <config-name><num-labs>

Example: Write in Command window this code "pmode start local 8" but we will get an error such as next figure.

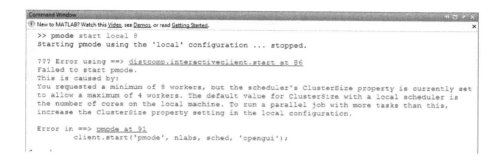

This error happened because we used the default configuration and it's set as 4 local as a maximum local, to solve this error we have to change the Manage configurations from a Parallel menu like the next figures, first step change the **ClusterSize** to 8 and press Ok.

Step two change the press **Star Validation** for applying this change and wait until get passed for all.

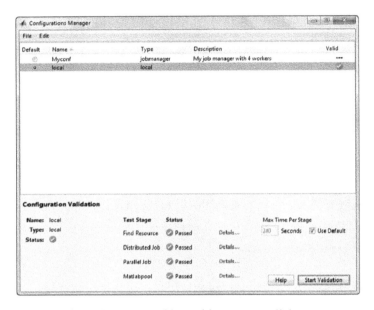

Now we can write the code to start with working as a parallel

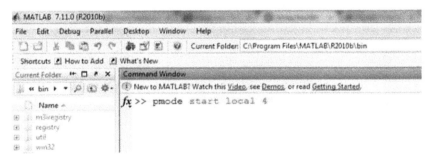

The next figure shows the Matlab window for 4 local also this figure illustrator what is the job of them.

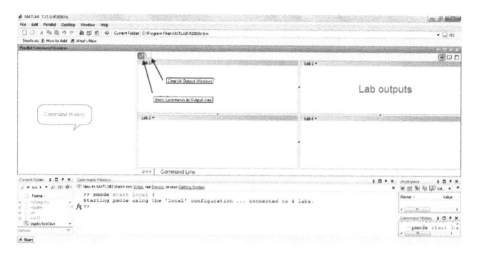

By using the propriety of each window you can change labs view , clear the code and you can get the history of your code from Command history.

Example : if you want write code to generate random number in Matlab use **Rand()** like

p>>a=rand(2)

You will get a different answer for each lab like next figure.

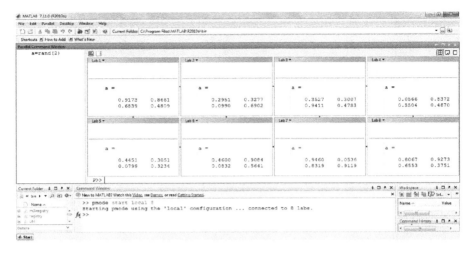

But if you write $p>>b=pi$ you will get the same answer (3.1416) for all

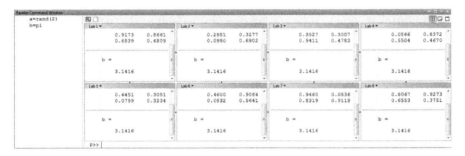

Sending and receiving data

If we want to send and receive the data between any labs we have to know which data want to send"Data sent to the other lab; any MATLAB data type" and destination is **labindex** of receiving lab . The syntax of send data is:

labSend(data, destination)

For receiving data from another lab we just need to the source address "**labindex**"

The syntax of Receiving data is :

data = labReceive(source)

Example: Generate a random number 'a' on lab 1 and send it to lab 3.

Solution : if(labindex == 1)

     a = rand(1)

  labSend(a,3)

end

if(labindex == 2)

   a = labReceive(1)

end

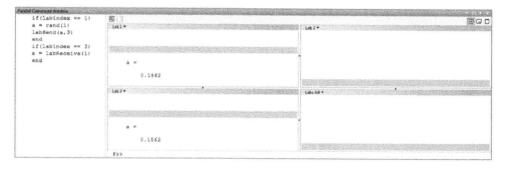

Example: Generate a random number 'b' on lab 1 and sends it to all other labs using a 'for' loop

```
if(labindex == 1)
   b = rand(1)
   for i = 2:numlabs
      labSend(b,i)
   end
else
   b = labReceive(1)
end
```

Example: Generate a random number 'b' on lab 1 and sends it after summation it with labindex to all other labs using a 'for' loop

```
if(labindex == 1)
    b = rand(1)
    for i = 2:numlabs
        labSend(b+i,i)
    end
else
    b = labReceive(1)
end
```

56

Collective communication

There are severl methods for collective communication between processors "labs" such as Broadcast,Gather,Scatter and Reduce.

1.Broadcastoperation

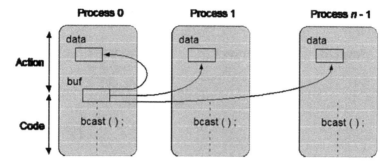

The Broadcast operation we will broadcast a value from one lab to other labs.

Example: Generate a random number 'c' on lab 1 and broadcast it to all other labs using labBroadcast

```
if(labindex == 1)
    c1 = rand(1);
    c =
labBroadcast(1,c1)
else
    c = labBroadcast(1)
end
```

Gather Opreation

In the gather operation we will gather values from labs to one lab.

can operate inside an **spmd** statement, **pmode**, or **parallel job** to gather together the data of a codistributed array, or outside an spmd statement to gather the data of a distributed array. We can use Gather operation such as

X = gather(A)

X = gather(C, lab)   %where A and C are the values

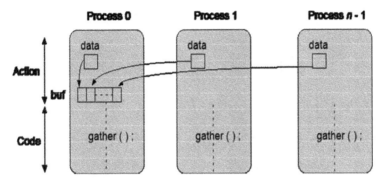

Example: Generate a random number 'c' on each lab and gather it to lab 1 using **gather**

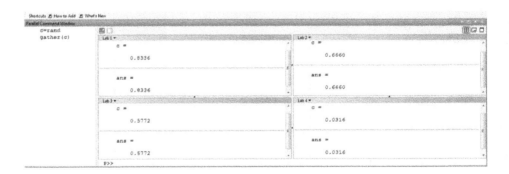

Global operations in pmode

The function res = gop(@F, x) is used to perform a global operation or reduction via the function F of the value x stored on each lab. The function F(x,y) should accept two arguments of the same type and produce a result of the same type so that it can be used iteratively, i.e. F(F(x1,x2),F(x3,x4)) is a valid expression. The function F(x,y) should also be associative, i.e. F(F(x1, x2), x3) = F(x1, F(x2, x3)).

As an example, suppose we generate a random value a on each lab using the command:

a = rand

Each lab will have a different value for a. We can find the minimum value across all labs and return the result to each lab using the command:

res1 = gop(@min, a)

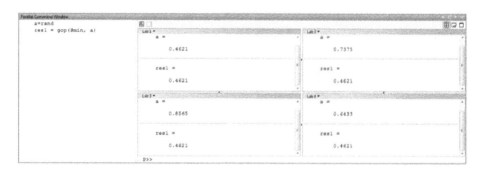

We can add all the values of a across the labs and return the result to lab 3 using the command:

res2 = gop(@plus, a, 3)

The corresponding Parallel Command Window is shown below:

59

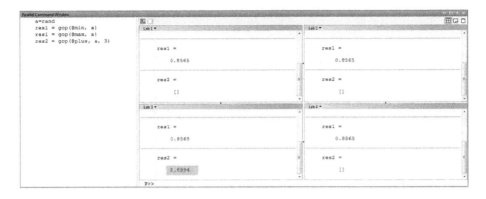

Distributed Arrays

The workers in a MATLAB pool communicate with each other, so you can distribute an array among the labs. Each lab contains part of the array, and all the labs are aware of which portion of the array each lab has.

First, open the MATLAB pool:

matlabpool open % Use default parallel configuration
M = magic(4)
MM = distributed(M)
M2 = 2*MM;
x = M2(1,1)

Now MM is a distributed array, equivalent to M, and you can manipulate or access its elements in the same way as any other array.

M2 = 2*MM; % M2 is also distributed, calculation performed on workers
x = M2(1,1) % x on the client is set to first element of M2

60

When you are finished and have no further need of data from the labs, you can close the MATLAB pool. Data on the labs does not persist from one instance of a MATLAB pool to another.

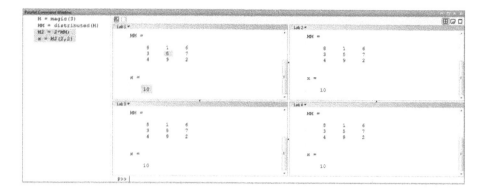

Single Program Multiple Data(pmd)

The single program multiple data (spmd) construct lets you define a block of code that runs in parallel on all the labs (workers) in the MATLAB pool. The spmd block can run on some or all the labs in the pool.

```
matlabpool    % Use default parallel configuration
spmd          % By default uses all labs in the pool
  R = rand(2)
end
```

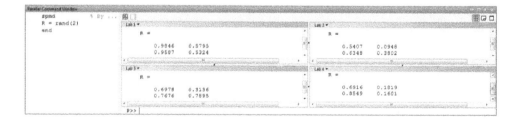

If we excute this code by using Matlab command we can see in the next figure the Lab4 give the result first, Lab1 , Lab2 the last one is Lab3 that means execute this code not sequentially but as a pool which lab is free at this moument execute first.

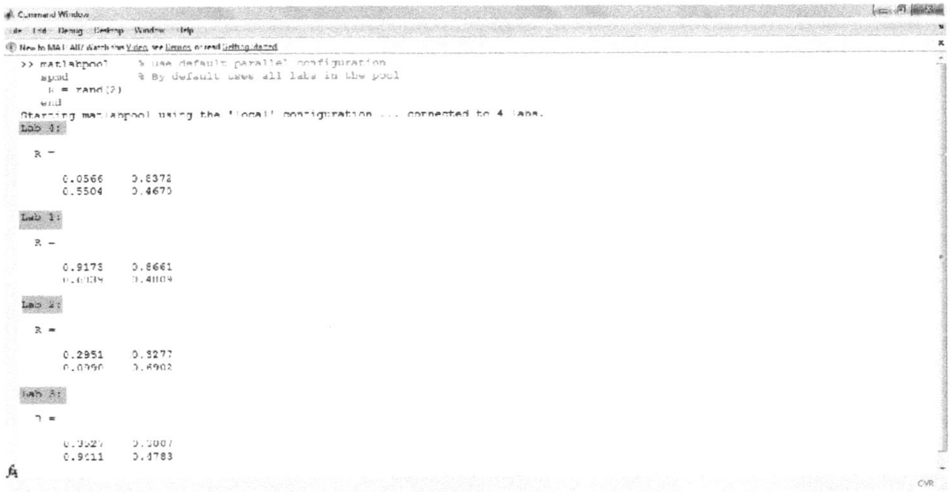

5

Matlab PCT with GPU

As we mentioned previously, PCT used in parallelism Matlab code and running this code using multiple processors but it still slow. For improving execution performance, the graphics processing unit (GPU) used with Matlab programming because the GPU is faster than CPU.The main capabilities of GPU are :

1. Transferring information between your Matlab and GPU card.
2. Executing Matlab code by using a GPU card.
3. You can use multiple GPU cards.

The GPU requirements

The main requirements for running Matlab code with GPU computing are :

1. The first requires is CUDA-enabled NVIDIA , you can use version GPU with compute capability 1.3 or above. Go to the following link to download it:*https://developer.nvidia.com/cuda-gpus*
2. Better to use the latest version of CUDA driver , for getting that , see (http://www.nvidia.com/Download/index.aspx)
3. Finally, the CUDA toolkit is not required for using the GPU computing functionality in the toolbox specially with PCT. But it is required just if you would like to build own CUDA kernels or MEX-functions with CUDA.

For more details about the requirments of parallel computing , please check mathworks group:

http://www.mathworks.com/products/parallel-computing/requirements.html

---

How to use gpuArray Data

We will describe the function by using some examples:

Transferring Data Between Matlab Workspace and Graphic Processor Unit (GPU)

Sending Data from Matlab to the GPU

For sending data from Matlab to GPU you can use the gpuArray function such as:

```
MM = 5;
N = magic(MM);
S = gpuArray(N);
```

Where S is representing the data of Magic square function, S which sorted on the GPU must be any data types such as (double, single, int8, logical,....etc.).

Retrieving Data from the GPU to MATLAB

For retrievingdata from GPU to Matlab workspace , you can use **gather** function such as:

M = **gather**(S);

You can check your data receiving correctly use **isequal**such as

DD= **isequal(M, your condition);**

Example: Create a XX random matrix with size 1024-by-1024 in MATLAB, and then send XX to the GPU and receiving this data from GPU to MATLAB :

```
XX = rand(1024);
GG = gpuArray(XX)
M = gather(GG);
DD= isequal(M, GG);
```
The result of example should be DD=1 that means the data which are sending and receiving same data.

Directly Creating GPU Data

A number of static methods on the GPUArray class allow you to directly construct arrays on the GPU without having to transfer them from the MATLAB workspace. These constructors require only array size and data class information, so they can construct an array without any element data from the workspace. Use any of the following to directly create an array on the GPU:

parallel.gpu.GPUArray.ones	parallel.gpu.GPUArray.eye
parallel.gpu.GPUArray.zeros	parallel.gpu.GPUArray.colon
parallel.gpu.GPUArray.Inf	parallel.gpu.GPUArray.true
parallel.gpu.GPUArray.NaN	parallel.gpu.GPUArray.false

For a complete list of available static methods in any release, type

methods('parallel.gpu.GPUArray')

The static constructors appear at the bottom of the output from this command.

For help on any one of the constructors, type

help parallel.gpu.GPUArray/functionname

For example, to see the help on the colon constructor, type

help parallel.gpu.GPUArray/colon

Example: Construct an Identity Matrix on the GPU

To create a 1000-by-1000 identity matrix of type int16 on the GPU, type

ii = parallel.gpu.GPUArray.eye(1000,'int16')

```
parallel.gpu.GPUArray:
---------------------
        Size: [1000 1000]
  ClassUnderlying: 'int16'
     Complexity: 'real'
```

With one numerical argument, you create a 2-dimensional matrix.

Example: Construct a Multidimensional Array on the GPU

To create a 3-dimensional array of ones with data class double on the GPU, type

G = parallel.gpu.GPUArray.ones(100, 100, 50)

parallel.gpu.GPUArray:

        Size: [100 100 50]
    ClassUnderlying: 'double'
      Complexity: 'real'

The default class of the data is double, so you do not have to specify it.

Example: Construct a Vector on the GPU

To create a 8192-element column vector of zeros on the GPU, type

Z = parallel.gpu.GPUArray.zeros(8192, 1)

parallel.gpu.GPUArray:

        Size: [8192 1]
    ClassUnderlying: 'double'
      Complexity: 'real'

For a column vector, the size of the second dimension is 1.

Examining Data Characteristics with GPUArray Functions

There are several functions available for examining the characteristics of a GPUArray object:

Function	Description
classUnderlying	Class of the underlying data in the array
isreal	Indication if array data is real
length	Return the Length of vector or largest array dimension
ndims	Return the Number of dimensions in the array

66

size	Return the size of array dimensions

Example, How can you find e the size of the GPUArray object:

GG = gpuArray(rand(1024));

SS = size(GG)

  1024   1024

Using Built-in Functions on GPUArray

You can use the Matlab built-in function on GPUArray, here I will provide you some of them for whole information go to mathworks on:
http://www.mathworks.com/help/distcomp/using-gpuarray.html

abs	bitand	diag	gamma	plus
acos	bitcmp	disp	gammaln	power
acosh	bitor	display	gather	prod
acot	bitshift	dot	ge	rdivide
acoth	bitxor	double	gt	real
acsc	cast	eq	hypot	reallog
acsch	ceil	erf	ifft	realpow
all	classUnderlying	erfc	ifft2	realsqrt
any	bitand	erfcinv	imag	rem
abs	bitcmp	erfinv	int16	plus

To get specific help of any functions, and to learn how to use you can do that such as:

help parallel.gpu.GPUArray/functionname

For example, to see the help of abs, type

help parallel.gpu.GPUArray/abs

67

How to select and identify your GPU device

For getting the number of CUDA devices you have to use the gpuDeviceCountfunction such as the following:

MyDevices = gpuDeviceCount;
MyDevices=
   2   here I have to GPU devices

For showing MyDevice propertiers,type

Properties:
                Name: 'Tesla C2050'
                Index: 1
       ComputeCapability: '2.0'
        SupportsDouble: 1
         DriverVersion: 4
     MaxThreadsPerBlock: 2048
      MaxShmemPerBlock: 49152
    MaxThreadBlockSize: [20482048 64]
        MaxGridSize: [65535 65535]
           SIMDWidth: 64
         TotalMemory: 2.8180e+09
         FreeMemory: 2.7591e+09
    MultiprocessorCount: 16
   GPUOverlapsTransfers: 1
  KernelExecutionTimeout: 0
      DeviceSupported: 1
       DeviceSelected: 1

Selecting GPU Devices

For selection the GPU device, type the **gpuDevice** function with inputs number for example: for selection device 2, type .

   gpuDevice(2)

6

Solving some problems in parallel using PCT

Sorting is one of the most common operations perform with a computer. Basically, it is a permutation function which operates on elements (Rahim Rashidy, 2011). A sorting algorithm is an algorithm that arranges a group of elements of a list in a certain order. Sorting algorithms are taught in some fields such as Computer Science and Mathematics. They differ in their functionality, performance, application, and resource usage (Altukhaim, 2003). In this assignment, we are using the old and common sorting algorithm, "Bubble Sort".

Bubble Sort Algorithm

Bubble sort is the oldest, the simplest and the slowest sorting algorithm in use having a complexity level of $O(n^2)$. Bubble sort works by comparing each item in the list with the item next to it and swapping them if required. The algorithm repeats this process until to make passes all the way through the list without swapping any items. Such a situation means that all the items are in the correct order. By this way the larger values move to the end of the list while smaller values remain towards the beginning of the list (Rahim Rashidy, 2011). In other words, all items are in the correct order. The algorithm's name, bubble sort, comes from a natural water phenomenon where the larger items sink to the end of the list whereas smaller values "bubble" up to the top of the data set (Altukhaim, 2003). Algorithm 1 shows the source code of the sequential bubble sort.

```
void bubble_sort (int x[], int n)
{
        int i,j;
        for (i = 0; i < n; i++)
            for (j = 0; j < n-i; j++)
                if (x[j] > x[j+1])
                    exchange (x[j],x[j+1]);
}
```

Algorithm 1. Sequential Bubble Sort (Rahim Rashidy, 2011)

There are some advantages of bubble sort which are: simple to program, easy to understand, quick to program, and low risk of having bugs. On the other hand its drawback are: inefficient, negatively affects its usability. Therefore it is still debatable among programmers whether or not to continue using bubble sort in practice (Altukhaim, 2003).

Example of Bubble Sort Algorithm

- Compare each pair of adjacent elements from the beginning of an array and, if they are in reverse order, swap them.

- If at the last one swap has been done, repeat step 1.

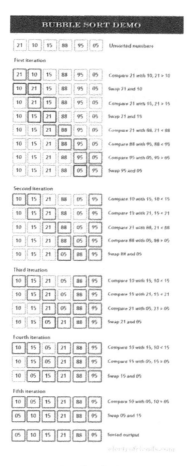

Figure 1: Example of Bubble Sort Algorithm []

Execution Bubble Sort Algorithm uses PCT

For executing Bubble sort on Parallel Computing Toolbox in Matlab we will use a text file which has 100 integer numbers (those numbers generated as random using Matlab) after that we will calculate the execution time for comparison.

```
function x=bubble(y)
m=length(y)
sorted=0; %flag to detect when sorted
k1=0; %count the passes
while sorted
    sorted=1; %they could be sorted
    k1=k1+1; %another pass
    for j=1:m-k1 %fewer tests on each pass
        if y(j)>y(j+1) %are they in order?
            temp=y(j); %no...
            y(j)=y(j+1);
            y(j+1)=temp;
            sorted=0; % a swop was made
        end
    end
end
%disp(x);
end
```

```
function Sorted = BubbleSort(A)
tic;
while 1 % loop indefiniately
c = 0;
for i = 1 : length(A) - 1 % each element except last
if A(i) > A(i + 1) % if current exceeds next
c = c + 1; % inc swap counter
t = A(i + 1); % store the smaller value in t
A(i + 1) = A(i); % assign the greater value -> swap
A(i) = t; % assign the smaller value <- swap
end
end
if ~c   % if no elements were switched
break;  % then break
end
end
tend=toc*1000
%$time=tend-tstart;
Sorted = A;
```

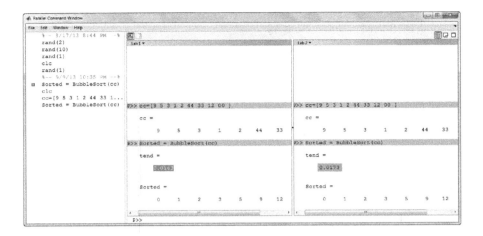

The previous figure shows there are different execution time the first core (lab1) sorted own list with **0.0163** and the second lab sorted with **0.0173**. That some time happened because there are many communication between cores.

REFERENCES

[1] Introduction to Parallel Computing , web site: https://computing.llnl.gov/tutorials/parallel_comp/#Whatis.

[2] G. S. Almasi and A. Gottlieb. 1989. "Highly Parallel Computing", Benjamin-Cummings Publ. Co., Inc., ACM, Redwood City, CA, USA.

[3] Parallel computing: available on , http://en.wikipedia.org/wiki/Parallel_computing#cite_ref-PH713_22-1

[4] Memory Architectures and Parallel Programming : http://www.dartmouth.edu/~rc/classes/intro_openmp/Memory_Architectures.html

[5] Introduction to MATLAB: http://www.gps.caltech.edu/classes/ge167/file/matlab_Resource_Seminar.pdf.

[6] Gaurav Sharma and Jos Martin , 2009 , "MATLAB®: A Language for Parallel Computing" , Springer, INTERNATIONAL JOURNAL OF PARALLEL PROGRAMMING ,Volume 37, Number 1 (2009), 3-36, DOI: 10.1007/s10766-008-0082-5.

[7] Moler, C., 1995, "Why isn't There a Parallel MATLAB" . The MathWorks Newsletter, Spring 1995

[8] Ashok Krishnamurthy, John Nehrbass, Juan Carlos Chaves and SiddharthSamsi , 2007 ," SURVEY OF PARALLEL MATLAB TECHNIQUES AND APPLICATIONS TO SIGNAL AND IMAGE PROCESSING" , IEEE.

[9] Ohio Supercomputer Center : https://www.osc.edu/node/306

[10] Intel iPSC/1, http://www.piercefuller.com/library/10166.html?id=10166

[11] Massachusetts Institute of Technology (MIT) : http://www.ll.mit.edu

[12] MPI standard: http://www.mpi-forum.org/

[13] Judy Gardiner, John Nehrbass, Juan Carlos Chaves, Brian Guilfoos, Stanley Ahalt, Ashok Krishnamurthy, Jose Unpingco, Alan Chalker, and

SiddharthSamsi. 2006. "Enhancements to MatlabMPI: Easier Compilation, Collective Communication, and Profiling". In Proceedings of the HPCMP Users Group Conference (HPCMP-UGC '06). IEEE Computer Society, Washington, DC, USA, 435-439. DOI=10.1109/HPCMP-UGC.2006.24 http://dx.doi.org/10.1109/HPCMP-UGC.2006.24

[14]   N.T. Bliss and J. Kepner, 2007, "pMatlab Parallel Matlab Library," To be published in the Special Issue on High Productivity Programming Languages and Models, Int. Journal of High Performance Computing Applications.

[15]   Ashok Krishnamurthy, SiddharthSamsi and Vijay Gadepally (2009). Parallel MATALAB Techniques, Image Processing, Yung-Sheng Chen (Ed.), ISBN: 978-953-307-026-1, InTech, Available from: http://www.intechopen.com/books/image-processing/parallel-matalab-techniques

[16]   William Smith, 2010 ," Matlab's Parallel Computation Toolbox", Mathworks.

[17]   N.T. Bliss , J. Kepner, Hahn Kim and Albert Reuther, "pMatlab Parallel Matlab Library," , ICASSP 2007, IEEE.

[18]   Interactive Supercomputing Corporation (ISC), 2007

[19]   MathWorks, http://www.mathworks.com/

[20]   MathWorks : GPU Programming in Matlab http://www.mathworks.com/company/newsletters/articles/gpu-programming-in-matlab.html

[21]   Introduction to GPU Architectures for HPC Computing, Michael E. Thomadakis, Supercomputing Facility Texas A&M University.

[22]   Introduction to GPU Computing, Peter Messmer , 2010, Tech- Tech-X Corporation

[23]   Parallel Computing Toolbox R2012b user's guide , 2012 , MathWorks.

[24]   GNU Octave: http://www.gnu.org/software/octave/

www.ingramcontent.com/pod-product-compliance
Lightning Source LLC
LaVergne TN
LVHW042344060326
832902LV00006B/379